# Female Problems
## An Unhelpful Guide

## by Nicole Hollander

A DELL TRADE PAPERBACK

A DELL TRADE PAPERBACK

Published by
Dell Publishing
a division of
Bantam Doubleday Dell Publishing Group, Inc.
1540 Broadway
New York, New York 10036

Library of Congress Cataloging in Publication Data
Hollander, Nicole.
    Female problems / Nicole Hollander.
        p.    cm.
    ISBN 0-440-50686-7
    1. Monologues.    I. Title.
PN6728.H58H65   1995
818'.5407—dc20                    95-16216   CIP

Printed in the United States of America
Published simultaneously in Canada

November 1995

10  9  8  7  6  5  4  3  2  1

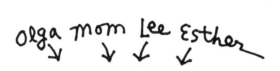

This book is dedicated to my mother
who had a gift for friendship.

I hope she's up there with her pals
chasing fires, visiting fortune tellers
and playing bridge.

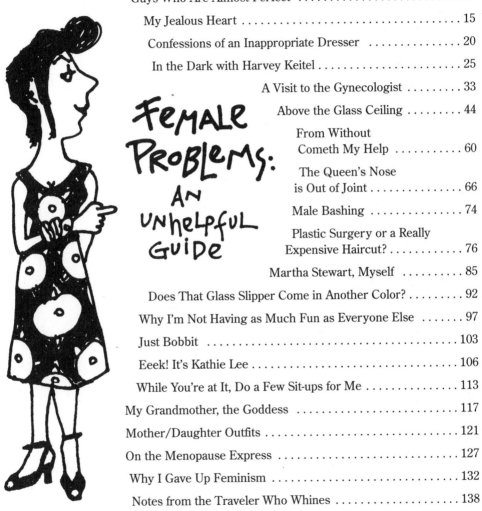

# Guys Who Are Almost Perfect

"How will you feel about being
married to a hunted man?"

"Oh, I don't mind."

— From *I Wake Up Screaming* with
Betty Grable and Victor Mature

He doesn't smoke or drink hard liquor. What does he drink? Well, you're going to laugh.

One of my favorite scenes in *Wolf* (with Jack Nicholson and Michelle Pfeiffer) is the moment when Jack has handcuffed himself to the radiator of his hotel room and confided to Michelle that he may be turning into a wolf. Michelle pooh-poohs the idea, suggesting that it might be just a brain tumor or something, which they can certainly take care of in the morning... and anyway, she's always dreamed of a good man looking at her the way he does.

So he has a little problem. It can be overcome or overlooked, managed... turned into a plus. Lots of men are flawed. So what if your guy is turning into a wolf, or in the case of *The Fly*, a very large lanky insect? Suitable men are difficult to find. Most women love animals.... Many of us were mad about horses in our adolescence.

I heard a woman in a pet store testify that her small, yippy dog gave her more pleasure than any of her three husbands. One day I admired the golden retriever of a young woman drinking coffee next to me and she announced with a contented smile, "My dog is better than any man I have ever gone out with. I have changed my life completely for him." I say men don't have to be walked every day — that is in their favor.

I don't personally know any women who would say they would change their lives for a man. It isn't done. I was shocked when a friend of mine took her husband's last name. It was understood in my mother's generation that women took their husband's name, proud that they had achieved marriage, and in addition they understood that men needed the sound of their women tap-dancing around them.... When the men were at home, that is. When they weren't at home they were the object of mimicry, and women's wit was honed at their expense.

Men no longer arouse that kind of sacrifice. If we have a good job in the East and they have a good job in the Midwest, then we marry and commute. But if your guy turns into a wolf, well, you've got to go with him — you can't go into couples therapy for it. Sure he's demanding, but heck, a wolf's got to do what a wolf's got to do. Perhaps more men would find their relationships with women improved by a wolf bite. Maybe women would cut men more slack if they had fur.... Maybe woman/canine is the next step in male/female relationships.

Personally, I still feel queasy about breaking that woman/insect relationship barrier. I've never had a pet bug. Of course, if my guy was Jeff Goldblum, maybe I could make allowances for his flyness.

# Bad Girl Chats

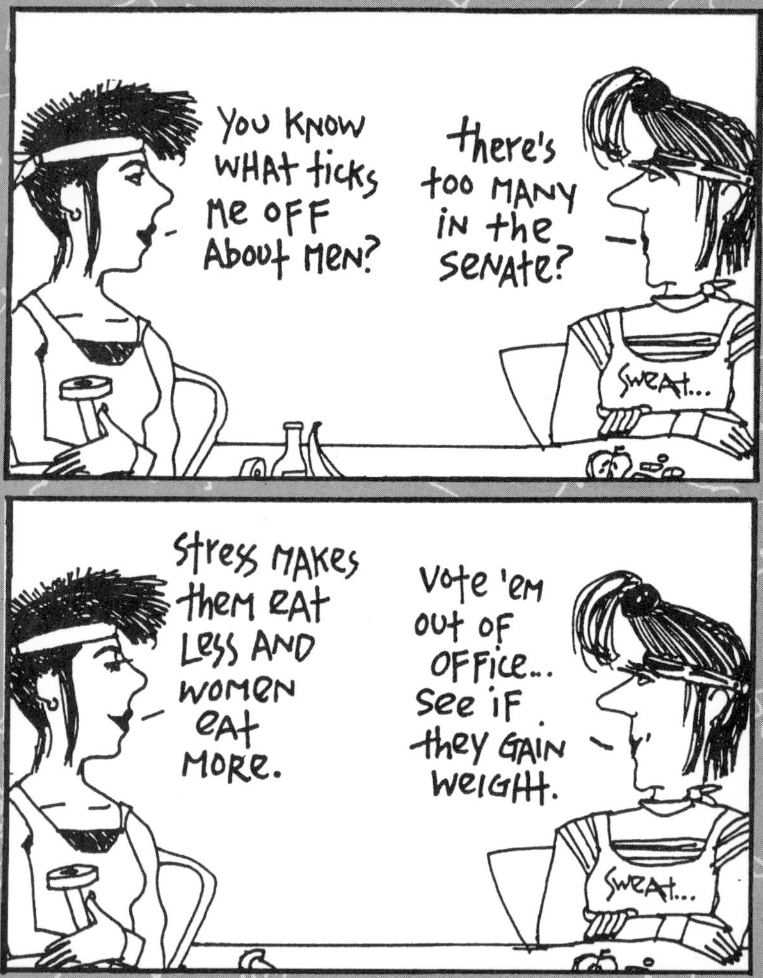

Alien Love: Can a woman raised on foreign films love a guy who loved "The Firm"?

The I.R.S. has targeted Hollywood. It's very unfair!

Don't take it so hard, sweet lips.

"Is this the gratitude your government shows the industry that gave us 'The Little Mermaid' and 'Jurassic Park'?" He asked sadly. "What if they promise to audit only the people who gave us 'Weekend at Bernie's II'?" I asked. "I loved that movie," He said in a shocked voice. The men of his planet have never seen a film they didn't want to see again, immediately.

Hi, Mom. You can't stop thinking about Burt and Loni? Yes, it's been difficult for all of us.

Why do I think they broke up? I know why... He wouldn't get hair plugs. Of course I made that up, Mom.

It was because he's a vegan and she's addicted to surf and turf. Yes, that's the truth.

What do you see?

People with high blood pressure are usually confident, happy with their lives, but have an increased risk of heart attacks and strokes.

Does this have any bearing on my date Saturday night?

Along with a lessened risk of strokes, low blood pressure brings tiredness, dissatisfaction and a low sense of self-esteem.

Wait, let me guess... My guy combines high blood pressure with low self-esteem?

You're psychic, right?

# My Jealous Heart

YOU DID WHAT?

*How are you feeling?*

How am I feeling? How do you think I feel? I've been in bed for almost two weeks; I feel dizzy every time I try to stand up; I'm coughing my guts out; my nose is blocked; I can't sleep because when I lie flat I can't breathe and when I sit up I can breathe but I can't sleep. My hair is dirty; my house is dirty; I'm behind in my work; I'm depressed. How do you think I feel?

*I have something to tell you.*

Well, tell me. You left me here alone for hours. I'm sick; I'm bored. What kind of a friend leaves a sick person alone for hours... doesn't tell me where she's going? And now you have that voice on you. Now I'm nervous. Tell me what you've got to tell me. Get it over with.

*I just slept with Robert.*

You just slept with Robert? You just had sex with my lover? In this building? With me lying here sick as a dog, dying for a cup of tea, my throat so scratchy I'd be happy to die right now, and meanwhile you're downstairs having sex with Robert? My best friend and you betrayed me — betrayed me while I had a fever. I can't believe it.

*I still like you better than him.*

Well, okay then.

# Confessions of An Inappropriate Dresser

*tennis anyone?*

A friend made me a wonderful hand-painted T-shirt. It was oversize, and fit me like a dress, except it was shapeless. I noticed that, so I put a belt on it. The closest I could come to matching the colors on the shirt was with a brown rubber belt that looked something like the ones we wore around our Girl Scout uniforms, only in rubber.

Then I put on little baby doll socks. They were given to me by a woman I didn't like, so there was really no excuse for them except they were also hand-painted.

Then I put on the little Mary Jane–type shoes that my cousin Gail gave me. Gail, who had come back into our lives after she had been ripped, at age two, from the arms of my aunt, the sister of her dead mother, by her father who came on the midnight train from California, and we never saw her again until she came to visit and bought me those shoes.

My friend Alicia was in town and we were going to an elegant restaurant for lunch. She looked at me and said, "Is that all you're wearing?" I chose to take her literally. It was summer. Of course it was all I was wearing.

What she meant was... "What, are you nuts? You're over forty and you're wearing an oversize T-shirt with a pair of funny shoes that have been out in the rain and hand-painted socks to a restaurant with a French name? Put on that little black dress with the polka dots."

But women are terrified to be direct. They don't want to hurt anyone's feelings. This handicap leads them into long affairs with weird men and the purchase of clothing they later regret. Perhaps our discussion could have led us to the revelation that worrying about whether we are properly dressed is an outmoded convention, but it was ten years too soon for that conversation.

Instead Alicia looked at me for a moment and said, "You look fine." I think I know what thoughts ran at the speed of light through her mind. "I am not her mother. Not that I would tell my daughter to change her outfit, because she would throw a tantrum and refuse to go to the restaurant and the whole day would be ruined. I have never seen Nicole throw a tantrum, but she could turn petulant and I have a restricted airline ticket — it can't be changed for under $500, so this is not the time to find out her true nature, and anyway, Nicole is an artist or at least a cartoonist, maybe it's okay for her to look goofy. Or maybe — and this is a horrible thought — what she's wearing is all the rage and I just don't know it because I'm stuck in a small town in Massachusetts where style is a foreign concept, which is totally my ex-husband's fault. I should have been back in California by now."

"No, it's fine," she says, and we go on to Monique's and give every woman there something to be grateful for... she's not wearing what I'm wearing.

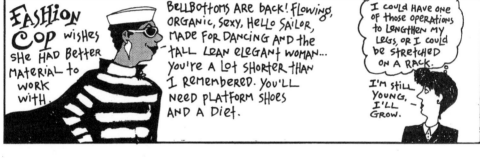

# In the Dark with Harvey Keitel

POPCORN. AND ERIC ROBERTS... SURELY I'M IN HEAVEN.

"I love *Casablanca*.... *Casablanca* is my favorite movie," said Linda.

"Yeah," Danielle said, "it's a great movie, but it's so sad."

"Sad? It's not sad. What do you mean sad? I love it when Humphrey Bogart and Ingrid Bergman walk off through the fog together — she's wearing that little suit that goes in at the waist — and he says to her, 'This is the beginning of a beautiful friendship.' Of course, it's sad for her husband because he has to get on the plane alone."

"Linda, excuse me, but she gets on that plane."

"Does not!"

Well, that's the way the film should have ended. I admire Linda for rejecting the unsatisfactory final scene of loss and sacrifice and substituting something upbeat. There's too much reality around anyway.

*The Piano* ended beautifully. And twice! (I can talk about final scenes because I know that every woman has seen *The Piano* and knows how it ends. I apologize to any woman who hasn't seen it because she was trapped in a car in the Swiss Alps during an avalanche or in a bad marriage, eating candy bars until her eventual rescue.)

The film seems to end when Ada and Baines get into a canoe to head for the ship that will take them to England. Okay, the canoe is a little unbalanced because they're carrying Ada's piano, but I'm not worried.

And when she insists they throw the piano overboard, I think, "Relax. It's a metaphor."

Then the boat tips. I tense, but it doesn't capsize and I begin to breathe again, and then the camera moves to her tiny booted foot caught in the coiled rope and she goes over with her piano down to the ocean floor and we stay for a long moment in the watery green with her, shocked, suspended in time, and then she slips out of her boot and we rise with her, cheeks unattractively distended, gasping for breath but triumphantly emerging from the sea. I was delighted. I didn't think it was one ending too many. I could have managed one more.

I wasn't troubled that Stewart, Ada's husband, takes a large axe and delicately chops off one, only one, of Ada's tiny fingers. The difficulty of a selective chop didn't cross my mind until some realist pointed it out...and it's true that a male director would have had her lose several fingers, if not the hand.

Jane Campion, the director, is one of us, so Ada loses just one dainty digit and Baines fashions her a silver finger stronger and more beautiful than mere flesh.

Willful, irritating, self-absorbed Ada gets her happy ending. Good for her. I know that when Ada learns to speak again Baines will be sorry, because she won't be limited by writing in pencil on those tiny pieces of paper. They will bicker; she will have the verbal edge; lust will wane, and she'll ask him to have the tattoo removed.... But looking ahead is always depressing.

Recently a friend and I passed a movie theater playing a double bill, *The Piano* and *Farewell My Concubine*. I turned to her and said, "Don't see it. They cut off a child's finger in the first scene." She wondered if the two films were shown together because of a finger-removal theme. We imagined a film festival involving the severed-body-part motif... and could one include that James Mason film that neither of us could remember the name of, even though he merely struck his student on the hand with a ruler when she played the piano badly?

I have always wanted to have a women's film festival, a festival of films with great roles for women, which I would hold in a tiny gemlike theater at the back of my bookstore/coffeehouse. I would show some of my favorite movie sex scenes. Two of my current favorites are the moment in *The Piano* when Baines finds a tiny hole in Ada's heavy black stocking and gently places his finger on her flesh; the other, of course, being the bedroom scene with Dennis Quaid and Ellen Barkin in *The Big Easy,* for its combination of heat and embarrassment.

I'd show great films with flawed endings. At the top of my list would be a little-known movie called *Coma.* The main character, played by Genevieve Bujold, is a smart and fearless young intern (early in the film she throws over her selfish young doctor lover, Michael Douglas, another point in her favor) who has discovered that some of her more senior colleagues are using their patients as organ farms, keeping them at a special facility where they are suspended, literally, in a half-life until they can be harvested.

My favorite scene takes place in a basement boiler room when Genevieve, chased by the evil doctor's minions, kicks off her pumps and climbs one of those vertical ladders they always have in the basement boiler rooms of hospitals so that the hero can escape through the heating ducts. She can't climb fast enough. Her feet keep slipping. It's those damn panty hose! She pulls them off and flings them away. Both she and Ada have this in common: they are triumphant over their shoes.

I often think of Genevieve flinging away her panty hose. I am not as fortunate as Linda, because I do remember the final scene of *Coma*. Genevieve is lying immobilized on a gurney, bound for the sinister Operating Room Number Nine where a twilight destiny awaits her.... In the nick of time she is rescued by Michael Douglas. That doesn't spoil the movie for me, but I feel in my heart that Jane Campion would have ended it differently. Genevieve would not have needed to be rescued by Douglas. She would have fixed her formidable eyes on the evil doctor and written on his mind, "Back off, you S.O.B.!" And he would have.

At the sound of the beep tell me which sex scene was best: the one in "the Name of the Rose" or "the Big Easy"?

Let's pretend you've just been to the movies and realize there are only two romantic fantasies open to women. Which one would you pick?

☐1. "I'm beautiful, young and have been a prostitute for about a week when I meet an emotionally stunted,

but darn good-looking corporate raider. I humanize him, and we stay in fine hotels forever."

☐2. "I'm a very hot 43-year-old waitress working in a hamburger joint who meets an emotionally frozen, really young account executive. He gives up his neurotic neatness and we have great sex forever."

Ma, this isn't your birthday.

The Birthday Fairy knows what you want and gets it for you.

All the more reason to celebrate.

Happy Birthday! I've arranged for you to sing "Making Whoopee" while perched on top of a grand piano, wearing a skimpy dress and 5" heels. Hurry, you can change in the limo.

Gee, I was planning to re-read all of Jane Austen...is Jeff Bridges waiting in the car?

# a Visit to the Gynecologist

wiTH the RiGHt AccessoRies EVEN tHat PAPeR GOWN you WEAR iN the exAMiNiNG Room...

CAN HAVe A ceRtAiN Je ne SAis Quoi.

A friend told me that once when she was at a gynecologist's, her feet in the stirrups, the doctor said, "I love your work." She felt that it was an inappropriate time for a compliment.

I don't think a sincere compliment is ever inappropriate, and anyway, it could have been worse. As she was inserting the speculum, the doctor could have said, "I know about you and my husband."

The point is, you don't expect a compliment during an internal exam. For most of us, the trip to the gynecologist is maintenance, like taking the car in for a tune-up, an activity best undertaken in a trancelike state. We hope to go through the visit engaging as little of ourselves as possible, and we do not wish to be told that our flywheel needs to be replaced.

When's the last time you wished you were going to see your gynecologist rather than going out to lunch? No, it's not something we look forward to. Perhaps compliments would help.... It might help to be positively reinforced while we're looking up at the ceiling or keeping our eyes squeezed shut.

What if, upon looking at your vaginal area, your doctor exclaimed (none of this works with male gynecologists, I'm afraid they'll have to go): "Wow, you have the most perfect labia I've ever seen and I've been practicing for twenty years. May I photograph them for an article I'm writing for the *New England Journal of Medicine*?" Or: "If Karl Lagerfeld or Romeo Gigli could see your vaginal lining, he'd design a fall line around the color." Or: "Did you know your cervix is patterned with a tiny constellation of stars? I believe that means you will be the next Dalai Lama."

You know what else would be nice? A manicurist in the examining room. You always have to wait in the examining room. The nurse weighs you and takes your blood pressure and then you're utterly alone. It would be pleasant to have your nails done while you wait for the doctor to make her entrance.

What about a pedicure during the actual examination? Your feet are up anyway. But perhaps that's going too far and succumbing to the pathological

modern need to do two things at once. You know, like talking on the phone and doing the dishes.

I'd like to have the option of watching a movie while I'm waiting. Every examining room should have a VCR and a selection of tapes. Just tack the cost onto the bill for the initial visit. We're used to an enormous bill for the initial visit — what's a few hundred dollars more? (I confess that most of my visits to the gynecologist are initial visits. I must be looking for the perfect gynecologist. Am I the only one?) There's no need to have an enormous library of videotapes. I'm sure many of us would enjoy seeing Richard Gere and Andy Garcia in whatever awful movie they're in, over and over.

Some of you out there are asking, "Why do we have to wait at all?" I always call the receptionist before an appointment and ask if the doctor is running on schedule and she always lies and says yes. What if she told the truth and we knew when we should show up?

I think that we have to accept that appointment time is a fiction. It's like asking someone if they like your hair. It puts them in a bad position. When you call to check on whether the doctor is running late, you're saying, "I trust you with my body, but I think you might be lying to me about time." Just go to your appointment as scheduled and sit in that windowless room on that uncomfortable chair and read those pathetic magazines.... After all, your doctor went to medical school and had to put up with a great deal. You can give her a few extra hours of your life.

I have one last request: Could you take down those baby pictures?

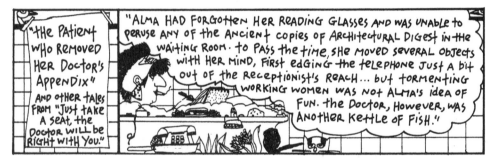

The woman who does EVERYTHING more beautifully than you belongs to a better HMO than you do, too.

Yesterday I took the children for a routine checkup. As usual, I was able to see the doctor immediately... I was sorry not to have more time in the waiting room, as they are well-stocked with new releases that have made the New York Times best seller list and fresh fruit. As usual, the doctor was caring and compassionate...and as usual, he handed me one perfect rose as I left the office.

Hi, boys. What's on your mind?

We were wondering if we have...

A HEALTH PLAN.

Yes. If you get sick, I will do absolutely everything to make you well, no matter what it costs.

How much is EVERYTHING?

EVERYTHING??

If only sheep gland injections would save you, I'd fly you to a clinic in Lucerne.

First class?

Would that be...

Now that it's summer, Love Cop is busier than ever keeping incompatible couples apart.

Remember... lust makes you stupid.

When I look into your eyes, I forget how nuts you are on the benefits of the Canadian-style single-payer health system over managed competition.

"Managed competition"... featuring mandatory enrollment in super HMO's—your doctor and hospital chosen for you—an untried theory beloved by insurance companies and heartless bureaucrats... and yet you're so darn cute.

Please step away from each other now or I'll be forced to hurt you for your own good.

**41**

# Above the Glass Ceiling

PROPS: *Large desk, chair, constructed ceiling with hatch, pointer, photograph in frame, dynamite, wiring and timing device. Golf club, tee, golf ball.*

*A young woman dressed in a boring little suit and boring little blouse is standing next to a desk bare except for a framed photograph and a coffee can full of pebbles. She's looking up at the ceiling. She reaches into the can and throws pebbles against the ceiling. (Speaks softly.)*

Yo, anybody there? *(Turns to the audience.)*

They never answer.

*(She puts a chair on the table and climbs up on it, then jabs the pointer all over the ceiling ferociously. She stops abruptly and looks at the audience.)*

Remember all those suspense movies where the detective is looking for the door to the secret passage? He figures the door's in the library. It's always in the library. He's tapping on the walls, listening for that special hollow sound. He feels around the carved fireplace mantel for the secret lever to the secret room, and then, frustrated, he leans back against the bookcase to light a cigarette and the hidden door springs open and he falls through.

*(She lights a cigarette, pokes the ceiling behind her with her pointer, not even looking at it, and we hear the sound of the hatch opening. She grins at the audience, turns and sticks her head into the hatch, and looks around. Taped sounds of low male voices, occasional male laughter. A mechanical voice shouts.)*

You're standing too close, move away. Intruder, intruder!

*(Sounds of men telling jokes.)*

So there was a rabbi, a minister, a priest, and a traveling salesman... *(or)* Did you see the bazooms on her?

*(To the audience.)* It's quite different than I imagined. I thought the other side of the glass ceiling would look like that place people see when they've died and are pulled back, somewhat reluctantly, to life... a long black

tunnel *(Mimes moving through the tunnel, feeling the sides.)* and way at the end you see a brilliant light and a door... and beyond the door... wildflowers... a meadow full of wildflowers and corporate executives.

The executives are smiling at me. They run to me, their thin hair blowing in the breeze, ties flying out behind them, glasses askew. They're elbowing each other out of the way, pushing and shoving to offer me the vice presidency, raising the ante until I'm all aglow with happiness.

*(Looks up at the hatch again.)* But it's not actually like that up there. There's a swimming pool, and there are little striped cabanas. Oh, and there's a bar. A woman dressed like Carmen Miranda is the bartender, wisecracking with the guys and making drinks, drinks with little umbrellas on them, lots of maraschino cherries.

So when you guys are all together, all you 95 percent white males — and there's no one around to see you — you have sissy drinks, right? *(Looks down and around the office and then up at the hatch.)* You realize this whole operation is being run by us down here, a bunch of women and people of color? Doesn't it make you nervous? Probably not. Probably makes you more nervous if we were up there looking at you all in your trunks — not a pretty sight, believe me.

*(Turns to the audience.)* You know, when I was a child, I dreamed of being a corporate executive. When other little girls were playing with Barbie dolls, I was pushing paper around on a little desk. Other kids had lemonade stands, I sold stock. When other babies were gurgling "Mama," "Papa," and spitting up, I was speaking in complete sentences. My first words were "Let's move the plant to Mexico."

My mother had to go into therapy. My father was secretly proud. He groomed me to be chief financial officer of a Fortune 500 company. We played Monopoly almost constantly. I dressed in little suits. I was always the first to arrive at school and the last to leave. Even then I was willing to work long hours.

I honed my managerial skills on hamsters. When I was ten years old, I had ten hamsters under me. I could make them march in formation, and they were happy too. I solicited their opinions. I relied on team management.

I went to Harvard, went to law school, got a business degree at Yale. I was on the journalism review. I read everything I could about corporate culture, and the place of women in it — rather a small, limited place... but I thought with my talents, I could succeed where other, lesser women had failed.

When I read that perfume on women was distracting in an office setting, I contrived to smell like the interior of a new car. I rubbed leather on this little hollow in my neck, behind my ears, and on my wrists.

Oh, and incidentally, I never cry. So for all those CEOs who are afraid to yell at a woman, don't worry, you can yell at me. I stand my ground. I won't run from the room. I trained myself. I used the G. Gordon Liddy method. Remember that guy who held his hand over a candle flame to make himself tough? Well, I didn't actually use a candle, I used a flashlight. But I didn't even wince. So I'm tough; but of course not too tough. My voice itself is quite melodious, not high, not low, not male, not female, sorta both at the same time.

I learned to speak the corporate language. My talk was spiked with metaphors of war and sports. When images female in nature came unbid-

den into my mind, I suppressed them vigorously. I might have said, "This deal is as wobbly as a giraffe in four-inch heels. This offer is to a real offer like Jenny Craig pasta is to linguine alfredo." I might have said, "I feel like picking up my panty hose and going home," but I restrained myself.

Speaking of panty hose, I find myself looking at the Victoria's Secret catalog more than I think a healthy woman should. I think dressing this way damages your psyche. And look at this office... this office is a model of masculine taste. *(Gestures around the office.)* Dark, woody... photographs of me landing a huge bass; my baseball cards; my moose head.

I allowed myself one picture on my desk, of my husband and children. Well, I didn't really have a husband and children; but I felt I needed a family to seem well-rounded, not like one of those neurotic women who gives up her entire life for the company and ends up nowhere. She looks around at age sixty-five and she hasn't even got a collection of Elvis plates from the Bradford Exchange.

But I digress. I was saying that I wanted to look normal. Did you know that in Japan, people hire family surrogates to visit their old parents and take them on outings? It's about $4,000 for a full day of togetherness. It's cheaper here, in the U.S. I once hired a husband and two kids for a dinner party at my house — it was $250 for the entire evening.

I daydream about business. When I close my eyes, I don't see myself on a windswept cliff, my long dark hair disheveled, wearing a low-cut blouse, held in the strong arms of a man with hawklike features... the two of us looking off at the horizon, panting heavily.

Nope, I daydream about the future. A future *(Puts her hand over her heart. Musical accompaniment.)* where American corporations are once again leading the way, grown strong and productive, unfettered by regulations that destroy their narrow profit margins.

I see Japan looking at us, biting their lips in envy. It's either save the environment or save jobs. I know what side I'm on. I believed Clarence Thomas. *(Winks.)* I know America can soar if we are totally free of the rules that govern a civilized society.

*(Stands up on the chair and yells into the hatch.)* I vote Republican, yet you block my advancement. I have brilliant ideas, yet you ignore them. This

THe Woman Who worries about everything worries about her fridge

Because the REFRIGERAtoR's USING ELECTRICITY 24 Hours A DAY It's POLLUTING the Atmosphere even WHILe we sleep...

MAYBE I SHOULD SHUt it OFF AT NIGHt AND put EVERYTHING Into A LittLe COOLER.

is my career, boys. *(Smiles, bows, genuflects.)* Forget the family benefits. Just give me a promotion. What do I have to do? Have a sex-change operation? *(Sniffs the air.)* Oh, now you're having lunch. Big Macs and fries, served by Ronald McDonald himself. *(Reaches up and brings back one french fry. Holds it up to the audience.)* Very nice, I'm sure. Eat saturated fat and die. No, look — I'm sorry I didn't mean to say that.

I pride myself on my ability to work with everyone. To think of the good of the company at all times. I am a team player. *(Rummages around in the desk drawers, brings out a little crumpled piece of paper, reads from it in a schoolteacher's voice.)* Twelve years ago, less than 3 percent of senior managers nationwide were women. Now women comprise less than 5 percent of senior executives. *(Crumples up the paper, tosses it away.)* That's the kind of statistic that could make a girl think of starting her own little company, making chocolate chip cookies with macadamia nuts or something.

But not me; I like batting my head against the wall. When I was a child, my parents were worried about me, because I derived a great deal of pleasure from banging my head slowly against my bedroom wall. Those early experiences are useful to me now.

Sure, I could take the entrepreneurial route. *(Shivers.)* The refuge of the corporately shunned, the lepers of the business world. I could become a big success, be interviewed on TV, make lots of money, give brilliant parties, have a full-time gardener, but it would be meaningless. I want to be accepted here *(Points upward.)* where it counts. I want to be part of a Fortune 500 company. It's my destiny.

*(Jumps down from the table, rummages around the trunk and finds a golf hat, puts it on and comes back to the desk with a golf club and a ball and tee. Sets the tee and ball on the table, gets back up, takes a few practice swings. Bangs on the ceiling with the club.)*

Let me in, you guys. I want to play golf with you. I think golf is an intellectually demanding game. It's all about strategy. It's like chess, only you wear plaid pants. Don't get me wrong. I love the outfits. I think golf should be an Olympic sport.... *(Bangs again on the ceiling with the club.)*

*(Speaker comes on. Male voices.)*

Please move away from the ceiling. Please move away from the ceiling, you're too close.

*(She looks up for a long moment and then shrugs... jumps off the table and reaches into the trunk again. Brings out dynamite, lots of wires and a timer, and a big staple gun. Pushes the dynamite up into the hatch and starts attaching wires and setting the timer. Sings softly.)*

"I'm going to wash that man right outta my hair and send him on his way."

*(Lights out, abruptly.)*

Sylvia's tips on Getting a job in a recessionary period.

Don't be a chump.

Interviewers may ask you to list your weaknesses in an effort to see how dumb you really are. Never say: "I have to have a nap every day at 3:00 P.M." Say something like "My biggest fault is I'm too much of a team player."

Sylvia's Post-Job-Interview Hotline

Is there something I can do after the interview to make sure I stand out from the other applicants?

Some experts suggest you write a brief follow-up letter after the interview, thanking the interviewer for her/his time, recapping your strengths and reaffirming your interest in the job. I think this approach is dead boring... Send a puppy.

Distressing Corporate Dreams

I dreamt I'd been working for this Hot-Shot law firm for about a year when I noticed that all the guys I started with had big offices and interesting cases, and I had all the boring stuff. So I went to one of the partners and complained, and he said, "Well, naturally you don't get the best cases, you're on the 'Mommy track!'" "But I'm a GUY," I screamed. "You people are so emotional," he said serenely.

**59**

# from without Cometh my help

I don't care for self-help. Seems kind of grubby and second-rate. I'd like something a bit more elitist. If I wanted self-help I'd get religion and live in a pretty convent. Although, come to think of it, that lifestyle is fairly

My therapist makes housecalls and my manicurist...if I could only get the vet to drop by.

No!

chock-full of directives from the outside. So now I'm stumped. I can't think of anything that smacks of self-help that I'd like to be a part of.

It's not that I don't need help. My basement needs to be scrubbed down, it needs to be painted... cleaned out. Broken and useless things have piled up down there.

Or maybe I'd like to get rid of a vice or a little personal habit too obscure and terrible to share with a roomful of people who innocently desire to stop drinking or wearing fur. I might need discreet, personal assistance.

I don't want to help myself. I want someone in here, in my house, in my face, helping me to conquer my faults. Or better yet, I want them to do stuff for me while I do something I'd rather do. I can think of many things I'd rather do than the things I have to do. No problem there.

So what I'm saying is that as we slip farther away from a manufacturing-based economy and head for one that is totally service-based, there will be a lot of opportunities for the creative entrepreneur. There's a whole new frontier out there. Step up, take advantage of the vacuum in personal services.

I'd like to look in the yellow pages and be able to order up a fun bunch to go to parties with me. I don't want to experience that initial awkwardness one has on entering a room full of strangers. It would be nice if my new pals also loaded up a plate from the buffet for me and, if necessary, rescued me from dull people as soon as the first sign of boredom flitted across my face. And they could steer me away from dangerous men and drive me home after the party and then take my car to the all-night car wash.

I could think of hundreds of special services. I could make a list right now off the top of my head. The only thing I worry about in this new service economy is how I'm going to afford to hire someone to fulfill these desires. But that's negative thinking. I probably need to get a little positive-gene therapy. Shape me right up.

# the Woman who worries about everything has an identity crisis

I WAS CARRYING A HEAVY SHOPPING BAG WHEN A YOUNG MAN CAME TOWARD ME ON ROLLER-BLADES. HE WAS WEARING A SHINY, SKINTIGHT JUMP-SUIT. I FELT MY ARM TWITCH.

It STARTED to SWING BACK AND FORTH FASTER AND FASTER... I WAS GOING to KNOCK HIM OFF HIS PINS! I MANAGED to STOP MYSELF. AM I A BAD PERSON?

HONEY, I'M SHOCKED.

# the Queen's Nose is out of Joint

SO, AM I still
the FAIRest
OR WHAT?

—OR WHAT.

My friends and I went to see the reissue of *Snow White and the Seven Dwarfs.*

I was horrified. One shouldn't watch movies viewed as a child after you've become a big irritable grown-up person. This time I hated Snow White. I saw her as manipulative and intent on getting her own way... a bland bimbo.

As a child I thought her good and beautiful, the victim of a cruel woman; now I see the poor Queen as the real victim.

The Queen is a damned sight more interesting than Ms. Snow White. Could it be my age? My allegiances seem to have changed dramatically. The Queen's mirror tells her she's not the fairest in the land. Well, I can relate to that. It comes to us all. Some of us retreat from the world. Some respond with fury and take it out on those close to them.

The Queen has Snow White to dump on. So she banishes her. Or does she arrange for the handyman to bump her off in the forest and he can't quite bring himself to do it?... I forget. I'm old. But since pretty young girls get all the breaks, Snow White ends up stranded in the forest but unharmed, and wanders into the home of the Seven Dwarfs.

Snow White is like one of those second sons who used to get pitched off the estate because the eldest son inherited everything. They became ministers or emigrated to far-off, exotic lands to make the locals miserable. Snow White imposes her values on the defenseless dwarfs.

Her values are limited, having to do mainly with housekeeping. And manners. Her standards of cleanliness are merciless. She dusts and cleans and cleans and dusts. The dwarfs are forced into service and the animals and birds of the forest impressed into her draconian cleanup gang.

She throws out the plates that don't match and institutes the use of damask napkins that have to be laundered after every meal. She teaches the dwarfs table manners and forces them to get flowered contour sheets.

She makes them kiss her before they leave for work. Yuck. And they seem to love it. Sellouts, sluts. Most of them, that is.

There's one holdout: Grumpy. Oh, dear Grumpy, we know you're doomed to fail, your bad attitude crumbling against the onslaught of Snow

White's aggressive cheerfulness. Perhaps the dwarfs welcomed her because they were tired of the same old routine. They were ready for novelty. "A change is as good as a vacation," or "It passes the time," as my mother used to say.

The dwarfs, poor besotted unattractive creatures, blossom under her bossy reign, or at least they bathe. Well, they hadn't seen a woman in a long time. Maybe they were old bachelors, maybe they were gay. I hope they reverted happily to their old ways after she was gone, because of course the little snip left them flat as soon as the prince kissed her rosy lips.

And I'm suspicious about that apple. I can't believe it was an apple that brought Snow White down. A fussy little number like that taking an apple from an unattractive old person? I think not. Probably had old person's cooties on it.

Probably it was not an apple, but a BLT. I know I'd be longing for a BLT if I was stuck in the forest.

I see Snow White wolfing it down and then the Queen reveals it was made with bad mayonnaise. Snow White laughs at her. She tells her mayonnaise contains citric acid and salt. It's not likely to go bad, even if it was as old as the old witch. Yow, that hurts.

Then the Queen offers her an orange soufflé that she's secretly prepared with out-of-date milk. As Snow White downs the last bite the Queen triumphantly shows her the date on the milk carton. Snow White is not impressed. She points out that the date merely instructs when the milk should be sold, not when it should be drunk. Damn!

Frustrated and beside herself, the old lady feeds Snow White oysters out of season, shrimp from polluted waters, poisoned portabella mushrooms, foods high in saturated fat.... It all slides off Snow White... she's got the constitution of a horse.

In desperation the witch hands her an apple. Snow White curls her lip and asks, "What's in this... ground glass?" The old girl is chagrined. She hadn't thought of that. She bites her lip and Snow White eats the apple and keels over. The Queen is delighted and puzzled.

It's possible Snow White just ate too much. Or she got into the dwarfs' sherry again. Just a temporary thing — she'll be right as rain in the morning.

The dwarfs are a bit premature in laying her out. Luckily, they don't bury her. The Prince arrives. He kisses her. She revives. The dwarfs, so mature, bid her a sad and gracious farewell. They don't even try to get cushy jobs in the palace. And what of the Queen? I hope the palace was in her name.

Here's my movie: The Queen's not looking in the mirror. She's at an upscale health-food supermarket, fingering the kiwis. She's used to admiring glances— men rushing to assist her, gallantry all around. When someone calls her "ma'am" for the first time, her fury is majestic, outsize — as befits a queen.

She doesn't bother to vent her fury on little Ms. Snow What. She destroys the supermarket, the New Age bookstore to the left of it, and the electronic discount outlet at the far end. Like a great maestro, she waves her wand and turns all the shoppers into golden hamsters.

Jamie, Grace and I decide to see "Snow White and the Seven Dwarfs."

the last time we saw Snow White, we were six years old.

And you made us late that time too!

We all get buttered popcorn, sticky candy and large cokes.

Is Snow white really insipid or is it just my imagination?

I think the Queen is over-reacting.

Hey Queenie, don't let the little twit get under your skin!

Could you shut up.

We get a little loud when we see the way Snow White manipulates the dwarfs.

Who told her she could just walk into their lives and take over? Those dwarfs are wimps. Suckers!

SHUSH!

Ladies, I'm going to have to ask you to leave.

It's about time.

We never see the end of the movie.

Jamie, Grace and I are asked to leave "Snow White" for talking too loudly.

It was still quite early. We decided to see another film or two.

Let's see how many Harvey Keitel movies we can see in one day.

We considered seeing "Reservoir Dogs" but it's nauseating, so we compromised by seeing "The Piano" for the fifth time.

Do you think he looks fat?

Fat and fabulous.

Now she's going to slap him.

SHUSH!

Could you put a lid on it?

Have you noticed how uptight people are in movie theaters?

I love this part.

Look out for that axe!

I'm going to have to ask you ladies to leave.

Want me to tell you the ending?

I hate you.

Luckily we were able to rent "The Bad Lieutenant."

How well do you know your Fairy Tales?

Mirror, mirror on the wall, who's the fairest in the mall?

I'm afraid it's that boring little Snow White.

How did the Wicked Queen put Snow White into that coma?

□1. Made her choose between a Chevy Blazer and a sweet little red convertible.

□2. Told her the dwarfs were just stringing her along.

WHAT MALLET?

# Male Bashing

A male reader writes that he likes my cartoons but has noticed some male bashing lately. This section is for him.

the Sylvia School of Scientific Writing
Bonus Phrase: "CORPUS CALLOSUM"

Students, sprinkle the Bonus phrase liberally in the story below.

"PAUL," I said, "DID you read that men's brains SHRINK 20% As they AGE?" "Doesn't matter, we're still smarter," He sneered, As he slapped on His baseball Cap, only to Have it slide down over His ears And come to Rest on His nose.

HARRY, COULDN'T I TALK ABOUT it A Little Bit?

I Don't WANt to Discuss the men's movement

NO.

EVEN iF I WAS very RESPECTFUL?

Leave it ALone, SYL.

I Never HAVE ANy FUN.

IF only that were true.

12 MEN INJURED IN DRUM Accident.

74

# Plastic Surgery, or a Really Expensive Haircut?

WILL NO ONE RID ME OF this HAIR?

My obsession with shoes pales beside my obsession with hair. As is often the case, it started in childhood.

About once a month my mother would greet me at the end of the day with her hair a different color than it had been when I left for school that morning. As a child I was disturbed, threatened by her inconsistency. Who was this woman with the dark brown hair — or, on one memorable occasion, green curls — and did she still love me?

Now, of course, I understand. Hair is the one feature we can change that utterly alters our image and yet doesn't involve surgery. (I saw a documentary on plastic surgery.... They peeled back a woman's face, took out some stuff, and then sewed it back on. I'll pass.)

Every time I sit in the chair at a beauty parlor I feel the same sense of excited anticipation. Wrapped in a sterile gown, my face innocent of makeup... I sense a new beginning. This time the stylist and I will become one, the whole more than the sum of its parts.

"Oh, yes," she will say, smiling. "I know exactly what you want. No need to speak, to spoil this moment with mere verbal communication... I saw your haircut in a dream last night."

This time I will be transformed, and without blood or pain or a recovery period in a Swiss sanitarium. My hair will have body, it will have movement... the highlights (not to mention the color) of childhood will reappear. Cleverly, the shape of the cut will make my nose appear more piquant, my eyes enormous. I will feel confident to speak in front of large groups and run for public office.

We are jaded. When it comes to relationships, we no longer expect a man or woman to change our life, but hair, hair is the final frontier... the land o'dreams. We can hope. We do hope at the hairdressers.

And when our hopes are dashed, we don't attempt to rip the face off of our hairdresser. Most of us don't. Most of us feel it was our fault, perhaps we didn't communicate clearly. We are women, after all; we own up to our complicity in our hair failure. Maybe next time.

Once, during a particularly bad period of my life, I walked into a beauty parlor where all the other customers were at least forty years older than me, and I let them cut and perm my hair.

That night my husband and I went to see *Lawrence of Arabia* and I wore a scarf on my head. I wore that scarf a long time, but eventually I was able to take it off. I didn't blame my hairdresser. I can't remember what she looked like. I do remember the next hairdresser I went to, because she was unkind. She looked at my hair and said, "If I had your perm I would kill myself."

But what if, as our society continues on its violent path, women are also infected by rage, directed not at themselves but at strangers?

What if they begin to carry guns and even to bring them into a hallowed house of beauty? Will we see headlines like: WOMAN GOES BALLISTIC, THREATENS HOSTAGES UNTIL HAIR GROWS OUT. DAY 75?

Will measures have to be taken to ensure the safety of stylists? Will the receptionist request that you check your weapons at the front desk, to be returned only after you've paid your bill and left a large tip and smiled at everyone? I hope it doesn't come to that.

WHAT REQUEST ARE YOU UNLIKELY to MAKE to YOUR HAIRDRESSER IN this LIFETIME?

□1. "Do MY HAIR LIKE MARILYN QUAYLE'S."

- THAT ABOUT COVERS it.

□2.

The History of BIG Hair

MARIE ANTOINETTE IS PLAYING SHEPHERDESS WHEN A STIFF WIND COMES UP. THROWN OFF BALANCE by HER HUGE HAIR SHE tumbles down the MOUNTAINSIDE. HER FALL IS BROKEN by SHEEP. LATER SHE IS GUILLOTINED FOR THE CRIME OF HIRSUTISM.

GASTON, OÙ SONT LES SHEEP?

YONDER, YOUR HAIRNESS.

there's A BOTTOM LINE FOR ALL OF US...

FASHION COP IS DEFIED BY A WOMAN WITH BIG HAIR!

the SMALL HEAD LOOK IS IN. I WANT to SEE YOU WEARING A SKULL CAP, KNITTED OR CROCHETED IN COTTON OR LINEN, this SUMMER.

OH, RIGHT, I'M GOING to PUT A STUPID CAP ON MY HEAD AND FLATTEN MY HAIR. I WOULDN'T WEAR A HAT IN A BLIZZARD, EVEN IF MY EAR FELL OFF.

MY HAIR WILL REMAIN UNFETTERED WHILE there's BREATH IN MY BODY.

# Martha Stewart, Myself

I FELT COMPELLED to BAKE HUNDREDS OF Cookies AND to Stencil the DOG.

"I was thinking of her when I thought of how Kathleen would look — and act, to a certain degree. All that pent-up energy devoted to crafts springs from a dark place, in my opinion."

—FILM DIRECTOR JOHN WATERS, ON BEING INSPIRED BY MARTHA STEWART IN DEVELOPING THE TITLE ROLE FOR KATHLEEN TURNER IN THE FILM *SERIAL MOM*, ABOUT A SERIAL KILLER.

I couldn't agree more.

The first time I saw Martha Stewart, I was idly watching television, as opposed to watching television and reading and eating at the same time, which I feel makes watching television okay. I was clutching the remote, because normally I don't care about cooking shows. I like them better than cowboy movies, but not much.

I once took a Chinese cooking class, memorable because of the wonderful food our teacher prepared and because we drank bock beer with that lovely food. I was always slightly buzzed after those classes. I had no intention of ever duplicating any of those recipes at home, but everyone was taking notes, so I did too.

A friend of mine, who was somewhat like Martha Stewart (only into sex, not crafts), borrowed my notes once. I explained to her that they were probably unreadable. I can't imagine why I gave them to her. Maybe I hoped they weren't as incoherent as I thought, or that she, being so perfect, could interpret them. They were covered with spots as well, and my friend was petulant when she returned them. They were pronounced illegible. I knew then that I was doomed to eat other people's creations and never receive compliments on my own, and somehow I have lived with that.

Anyway, Martha was making a French dessert when I tuned in, and in a matter of minutes her intensity had pinned me against the wall and had loosed the remote from my nerveless fingertips.

This French dessert, this croquenbouche, involved constructing hundreds, maybe thousands, of tiny cream puffs, filling each with a chocolate espresso cream — injected into the puffs with a 1/4-inch pastry tip — then individually dipping each puff into caramel syrup and piling the puffs higher and higher into a towering pyramid and then, using a modified balloon whisk (Martha modified that balloon whisk right in front of me with huge steel clippers.... My hands were shaking. No man could have watched it.), whirling cobwebby strands of caramel around and around the pyramid until the whole creepy edifice would not have been out of place in *Great Expectations* on Miss Havisham's nuptial table — the table that's been right there in her room lo these many years with the food untouched and petrified since she was jilted on her wedding day.

I've loved Martha ever since I first saw her. I love Christopher Walken too. But I don't need to have dinner with either of them.

Alien Lovers. CAN Love SurvivE bENDING OVER A Hot StoVE ON A FAR DiStaNt PLANEt?

DEAREST, I'D Like to invitE somE of our NEiGHBors oVER FOR A REAL tHANksGiViNG DiNNER.

OH, AND WHO'S GOING to cook this DiNNER?

SiNcE MOViNG to VENUS, I'D tAkEN A VOW OF NO COOkiNG AND HAD ONLY A VAGUE idEA OF WHERE the KitchEN WAS. "It would MAkE ME SO PROUD IF YOU'D COOk," HE SAiD kiSSiNG ME FROM ANkLE to EAR. "OH, ALL RiGHt," I SAiD, WONDERiNG iF I could GEt MARtHA StEwARt to WHip up the DiNNER iF I GAVE HER ExCLUSiVE RiGHtS to the StORY AND PROMiSED SHE would APPEAR iN EVERY PHOtO.

DO YOU tHiNk...

MARtHA StEwART DRiNks MiLk...

RiGHt out of the CARtON?

the WomaN whose Life is MorE BEautiful and OrgaNized than Yours, writes in her Journal about StrEss.

PEOPLE tHiNk tHAt A WOMAN LiKE ME, WHO HAS bEEN PERFECTLY ORGANiZED SiNcE iNFANcY, would NEVER bE iNcONVENiENcED by StRESS. tHAt ticks ME OFF. JUSt LASt wEEk, I ExPERiENcED StRESS. the CHiLDREN AND the GARDENER HAD to WRAP ME tiGHtLY iN HEAtED HERBAL BLANkEtS AND PLACE ME iN A DARkENED ROOM, WHERE I LiStENED to WAGNERiAN OPERAS UNtiL I WAS MYSELF AGAiN.

NOW BEGIN STACK-ING THE 350 CREME-FILLED PASTRY SHELLS ON A FOIL-COVERED CARDBOARD CIRCLE, USING THE SUGAR CARAMEL SAUCE THAT HAS BEEN SHAKEN bUT NOT STIRRED TO AVOID CRYSTALLIZATION, INTO A PYRAMID.

THEN, USING A WHISK THAT'S BEEN MODI-FIED BY SHEARING OFF THE bOTTOM WITH WIRE CUTTERS, SPIN THE REMAIN-ING SAUCE INTO THREADS TO FORM A WEB THAT WINDS AROUND AND AROUND THE PYRA-MID OF CREME PUFFS UNTIL IT...

UNTIL IT LOOKS LIKE SOMETHING MISS HAVISHAM MIGHT HAVE FORCED YOUNG PIP TO EAT.

I WORSHIP MARTHA STEWART.

THE Woman who does everything more Beautifully than you writes about it in her journal.

TUESDAY - SPENT THE MORNING AGING MY TERRACOTTA POTS FIRST DIPPING THEM IN A MIXTURE OF MY OWN HOME MADE LOW-FAT YOGURT WITH CUMIN AND THEN WRAPPING THEM IN A PLASTIC BAG AND STORING THEM ON THE BACK SEAT OF AN OLD BUICK. THEY SHOULD COME OUT IN A FEW DAYS LOOKING LIKE THEY WERE DISCOVERED IN THE RUINS OF A 15th-CENTURY PALAZZO. I HATE NEW TERRACOTTA, DON'T YOU?

THE WOMAN WHO DOES EVERYTHING MORE BEAUTIFULLY THAN YOU GETS THE CHILDREN READY FOR THEIR RETURN TO SCHOOL AND HAS TIME FOR A FEW GOOD WORKS.

SUNDAY. MONOGRAMMED THE CHILDREN'S UNDERWEAR AND COLOR-COORDINATED THEIR SCHOOL OUTFITS FOR THE YEAR. JOHN, OUR WONDERFUL HANDYMAN, MADE THEM LOVELY PENCIL CASES FROM OUR OLD BARN, RECENTLY STRUCK BY LIGHTNING. WE'RE USING THE REST OF THE WOOD TO BUILD AN ADDITION TO THE LOCAL PET SHELTER AND A PLANETARIUM IN THE BACKYARD.

the Woman who Manages Her time So much better than you do Writes in her Journal About Cable television.

I WAS APPROACHED BY ONE OF THOSE CABLE COMPANIES OFFERING TO INSTALL CABLE TELEVISION IN MY HOME, FREE, FOR ONE MONTH. WELL, I WAS AMUSED BECAUSE, OF COURSE, WE DON'T OWN A TELEVISION SET. OUR FAMILY EVENINGS ARE SPENT READING ALOUD TO ONE ANOTHER, SINGING OUR OWN COMPOSITIONS AROUND THE GRAND PIANO, OR MAKING LACE.

the Woman who does Everything More beautifully than you turns her Hand to good Works.

TUESDAY: YESTERDAY THE CHILDREN AND I HELPED OUR ELDERLY NEIGHBORS' GOLDEN RETRIEVER DELIVER HER PUPS. BY THE AFTERNOON WE HAD PLACED ALL OF THEM IN GOOD HOMES AND GOTTEN ONE A T.V. CONTRACT. TOMORROW, OFF TO THE STATE PRISON TO TEACH THE INMATES TO PREPARE MICROWAVE RISOTTO!

the Woman who does everything more Beautifully than you does Christmas Better than you, too.

CHRISTMAS DAY, 7:30 A.M. THE GIFTS HAVE BEEN OPENED... OH, HOW DELIGHTED EVERYONE WAS WITH THEIR HANDKNITTED CASHMERE SWEATERS MADE OF CASHMERE COMBED, NOT CUT, FROM THE GOATS OF A CHARMING TRIBE OF SHEPHERDS I MET ON MY LAST TRIP TO INDIA. THE WRAPPING PAPER AND THE CHRISTMAS TREE HAVE BEEN DROPPED OFF AT THE RECYCLING CENTER, AND THIS AFTERNOON WE START ADDRESSING NEXT YEAR'S CARDS.

# Does that Glass Slipper Come in Another Color?

Look, I KNOW you're MY FAIRY GODMOTHER AND you're DOING ME A REALLY bIG FAVOR, bUT...

Well, all women love shoes, don't they? If you love shoes and think your hair looks bad pretty much all the time, you're a woman.

If we saved all our shoes, we could write the novel of our life by looking at them. Didn't that Frenchman do it with a cookie? We'd remember everything. But you can't save a shoe with a pointed toe, dyed peach to match an unattractive bridesmaid's dress. Once a shoe goes out of style you have to get rid of it. You can't let it sit on the shelf and mock you. There's nothing more pitiful than a woman at a shoe repair shop trying to update a pair of boots with a stacked heel that resembles wood. It can't be done.

It is our acceptance of what we cannot change that allows us to go on to maturity and other styles. By the same token, when you look in your closet and see a pair of shoes that causes you pain, you must remove them from your closet and your life. Admit that you knew when you bought them they didn't fit...would never fit, that stretching them was futile. But you brought them home anyway. You lost the sales slip immediately and then you defiantly wore them outside and made them nonreturnable.

You listened to the inner voice that said, "I can make these shoes fit me." It's the same voice that says, "I can make this man fabulous."

Which brings me to Cinderella, the ultimate shoe story.

Cinderella's at the ball, the clock strikes midnight, and she runs off, leaving her glass slipper on the palace steps. The Prince frenetically searches the kingdom for her, and when he finds her and slips the glass slipper on her foot, she takes him to her closet and shows him her collection of Birkenstocks.

The Prince tries to be polite. He's well brought up, but he's terribly bored. "Very nice, I'm sure," he says, but his eyes get that glazed look the way guys' eyes do when they find themselves in the women's section of a shoe store.

Cinderella: "You don't like shoes?" (Women are sensitive to that look.) "That's funny — I heard you liked shoes. They told me, 'Go to the ball, catch his eye, and then run off leaving a high-heeled pump behind. The guy will go bananas. He'll run all over town looking for you. He'll hire servants full-time to check out leads, new jobs all around. Every time a good-looking woman leaves a shoe behind on the palace steps it's great for the economy.... But make sure the shoes have a real high heel — he's a freak for high heels.'"

She opens another closet — this one with dressy shoes — and says to the Prince, "If you want high heels I've got high heels, but I can't wear them all the time. They shorten the calf muscles."

And they lived happily ever after.

Alien Love * CAN AN EARTH WOMAN keep Love ALive WITH A Sweet-NATURED ALien, even tHoUGH SHe LOATHES His PALS? 🐱 ✶

I'M SO RELIEVED. IMELDA'S HER OLD SELF. AGAIN.

Swell.-

"SHe went SHoppinG iN HoNG KONG AND bouGHt 6 pAirs of crocodile sHoes for $5,806.00!" He SAiD HAppily. "BiG DEAL," I Snorted. "the woMAN'S prActically A sHoe FetisHist... SHe'D buy sHoes 5 Minutes before the ApocALypse..." I PAUseD to tAke A breAtH AND NoticeD His Lower Lip treMble. the MEN of His PLANet ADore IMELDA. "OKAY, OKAY. I'LL INViTe HER AND the BucHANANS for DiNNer reAL sooN," I SAiD, BitiNG MY Keds.

Cinderella's Foot slid EASily into the Glass slipper.

"Now we CAN Live HAppily ever AFter."

"ActuALly, PriNce,"

SAiD CiNderella, "I usuALLY weAr BirkenstocKs, tHAt is, iF I'M Not plANNinG to wALK, in wHicH CAse I'D weAr soMetHinG tHAt ties up the FrONt witH GooD ArcH support. Let Me sHow you MY sHoes," sHe SAiD GAiLY, tAkiNG the GLASSy-eyeD PriNce by the HAND AND LeADiNG HiM to HEr Closet.

soMeDAY My PriNce wiLL coMe...

IN the NEAR FuTure, there wiLL be 500 CABLE cHANNELS. WHAT KiND of proGrAMs woulD you Like to see? □1. "A HoMe sHoppinG Network wHere you CAN Buy sHoes 24 Hours A DAY."

□2. "the ALL-FooD cHANNEL: COOKiNG sHows, olD Movies witH pie tHROwinG, AND sHort poetic seGMents FEATuriNG sAusAGe AND eGGs... No diALoGue, Just the eGGs FroM DiFFerent ANGLes."

MA, Are you BrooD-iNG?

the Woman who worries about Everything is Happy when she can take a worry off her list

I JUST HEARD THAT SOMEONE DONATED $20 MILLION to YALE UNIVERSITY FOR A NEW ELECTIVE COURSE OF STUDIES IN WESTERN CIVILIZATION. I'M SO GLAD! MANY'S THE NIGHT I'VE...

LAIN AWAKE WONDERING WHERE YALE WAS GOING TO GET THE MONEY FOR MORE COURSES IN WESTERN CIV.

HONEY, SARCASM DOESN'T BECOME YOU.

# Why I'm not Having as Much fun as everyone else

**I wear A beret AND yet I'M UN-HAPPY**

I suffer from a low-level depression, a certain lack of joie de vivre. I had my metabolism tested, I flirted with exercise, I wrote briefly in a journal. I explored the popular antidepressant drugs. I wasted many hours with friends analyzing my ennui and adding to theirs, without coming any closer to the source of my problems. And to think the answer came to me in Indiana, in front of the TV. Yes, my epiphany, or rather my *coup de foudre,* came while drinking a glass of champagne and watching a tape of Marguerite Duras's *The Lover.*

I called out to my friends, "Oh my God, I can't believe it. This is my life." I alerted them to the stunning parallels between Marguerite's experiences and mine. (They could have been smoking opium for all the response I got.)

Perhaps you will be more interested.

As a young girl with a fondness for hats, Marguerite had an unforgettable love affair with a handsome Chinese man who was twice her age, who married someone else although he loved only her all his life, and who had a little drug problem. *Moi aussi*. Me too! My love's drug of choice was not opium but something less romantic in pill form — it was a different time. At any rate, Marguerite Duras made a book and a major motion picture out of her experience and I don't have so much as a photograph, or even one of the many pairs of lovely cowboy boots he owned.

Or take the case of Simone de Beauvoir — writer, philosopher, and serious person. She had an affair with Nelson Algren in Chicago. After her affair she wrote a novel — *The Mandarins*. Nelson Algren was a Chicagoan. I am a Chicagoan. I've had affairs with men in Chicago who were also from Chicago. Yet I have no novel to show for my experience.

Marguerite, Simone, Nicole. Our names are so similiar. Of course! *(Sound of hand hitting head.)* They are French. I am not.

How else to account for my own lack of an oeuvre or even a novelette? I see it clearly now. My parents named me Nicole, thinking it was enough to ensure me an interesting life or marriage to a professional man. In fact it barred me from the mundane without propelling me into the exotic. A half-life if there ever was one. No wonder I feel tired all the time. To name me after the French heroine of an American film called *The Rage of Paris* was a woefully inadequate gesture. It simply set me up for failure. I am non-Gallic. A nonstarter in the seriousness sweepstakes. This is the core of my problem. It is why after the age of fourteen I stopped being amused by Jerry Lewis and why I had to marry a man with an accent — of the wrong kind.

I did not go to a Catholic girls' school called Merciful Sisters of the Sacred Bloody Bleeding Heart like Simone De Beauvoir or even like many of the other girls in my neighborhood did. I went to a public school and it was called Delano, after Franklin Delano Roosevelt. As a consequence, I have been a lifelong New Dealer, well after it went out of fashion.

I feel sure that attending a Catholic girls' school or even a boarding school would have led me to acts of rebellion, exciting sex, and a major in philosophy. My parents erred twice: not only in being non-French, but in being non-Catholic.

Wait. What if my parents had not been French, but Catholic and athletic, the way Grace Kelly's parents were? And if I was the outsider daughter like Grace, the one who didn't leap off the garage, or the high diving board? (And certainly I would have been that daughter.) I might have grown up to marry the Prince of Monaco and become princess of a country where they at least speak French. Instead, I married a man who spoke Hungarian, the stuff of farce, not tragedy.

And even if my parents had not been athletic or French or Catholic but one of them merely a famous actor... I might have married a French director like Roger Vadim and been like Jane Fonda — silly and then very serious and then married to Ted Turner and into my spiritual side. As it is, I don't think I even have a spiritual side.

The more I think about the root cause of my unhappiness, the more murky and tangled the whole business becomes. Is it my lack of Frenchness or Catholicity or perhaps my Midwestern birth or my physical stature or an insurmountable combination of genetic and environmental factors that has robbed me of the fun that everyone else has in gobs? Of course, knowing it was not my doing — knowing that the deck was stacked against me — gives me some comfort. It's clear none of this was my fault, Mom.

HONEY, I'M HOME!

# Just Bobbit

A few years ago the *Village Voice* asked me to submit a cartoon for their "year in review." I did. They rejected it, but they asked me to do another one, perhaps more focused, perhaps more biting, I wasn't sure.

I had been thinking about the female condom and I thought I would do the cartoon about that, but I would do it in the form of a fairy tale: Cinderella.

I hadn't actually seen a female condom, since in the United States, where I live almost every day of my life except when I leave my body, you need a doctor's prescription for one, and I felt that this was going too far for a joke. So instead I went to England where you can purchase them over the counter in any chemist shop and buy some pretty nice lipsticks at the same time.

I got the Femidom brand of female condom, and I read the instructions, since I had no idea from looking at the thing which end went into which body.

It comes in a three-pack. I took one out. It was covered with goo, which I got all over my hands. I passed it along to a friend. There was enough goo left to cover her hands as well. I noticed that when I handed it to her, she held it at some distance away from her body and made a tiny moue of disgust.

When I got back to the States I showed the Femidom to a number of women friends and they all held the condom away from themselves and pursed their lips in the very same way. My pharmacist, also a woman, said she thought the opening for the male genitalia was rather large — I think she said something like, "As if."

Anyway, I submitted my condom cartoon to the *Village Voice* and they rejected it, but they asked if I would give it one more try and do a cartoon about the woman who cut off her husband's penis. I demurred. I guess I just wasn't feeling up to it.

# Eeek! It's Kathie Lee

WHAt
WAS
tHAt
Noise?

I fear exercise, flying, great heights, walking around alone at night, musical comedy, small dark places, roaches and mice, cash machines that run out of money, sudden noises, new neighbors, cocktail parties, foreign languages, stolen credit cards, credit bureaus, the IRS, bombs at airports, airline food, bingo, stuffing from inside the turkey, dentists, highway construction, vicious dogs, gangs of eight-year-old boys, nursing homes, dense forests, getting locked out of my apartment without shoes, deserts, empty highways, pierced nipples, abandoned motels, running out of gas, miniskirts, spiked heels, mold, Republicans, killer bees, spit on the sidewalk, Fundamentalists, graffiti, snowstorms, cold weather, humidity, gum disease, telephone calls after 9:00 P.M., large bodies of water, people who talk a lot, mysterious tinfoil packages in the back of the refrigerator, the FBI, shy people, washing machines that overflow, frozen pipes, walking across an open field during a thunderstorm, ant invasions, piles of ironing, sudden attacks of lust, electrical outlets, tomatoes without flavor, mobile homes during a hurricane, runaway horses, maps, cruise control, hockey pucks, masseuses who crack your neck, getting trapped in a sauna, car jackers, men in suits, crying babies, cruel landlords, crooked mechanics, Freddy Krueger, insurance companies, needles, tongue depressors, plastic bags, and Florida.... **But please, O powerful one, O ruler of the body, please don't make me fear hot dogs with everything, on a poppyseed bun; ice cream laced with chocolate and nuts; thick steaks; garlic bread with butter; two eggs over easy with bacon, hash browns, and a side of sausage; or meat loaf with gravy.**

# While you're at it, do a few Sit-ups for Me

Have you seen that cartoon of a scientist walking in front of a line of ducklings? They think he's their mother. Early imprinting. I'm sure it's easier to make a duckling believe a man in a white coat is her mom than to make some people think they like to exercise. You can probably teach children to like exercise if you start them young enough, like in utero.

I'm surprised someone hasn't thought of marketing exercise tapes for the fetus... water aerobics, synchronized swimming, the Esther Williams Fetal Ballet. It might have helped me. My mother could have played the tapes while she smoked those long cigarettes. I suppose that proves it can't be done. If you could influence a child in the womb, I would have come out blowing smoke rings.

As it is, there's no hope. I find no reason compelling enough to make me exercise. And I've tried. I am a woman. I have tried.

I have heard people say that once you exercise you miss it when you stop. I am living proof of the wrongness of that statement. I exercised. I stopped. I never looked back.

There is no music, no book on tape, no image of a taut body strong enough to keep me on a StairMaster. Perhaps if it were the StairMaster or prison... I don't know. It's not that the StairMaster is more boring than other exercise and it's not that I don't appreciate boredom. I revel in it. But I'd rather not be doing leg raises while I'm bored. I'd rather be watching John Tesh on *Entertainment Tonight*. Don't tell me I could be doing sits-ups and watch John Tesh, because that verges on the cruel.

We have a genetically altered tomato. We will have genetically altered bodies. I'll just wait.

# Bad Girl Chats

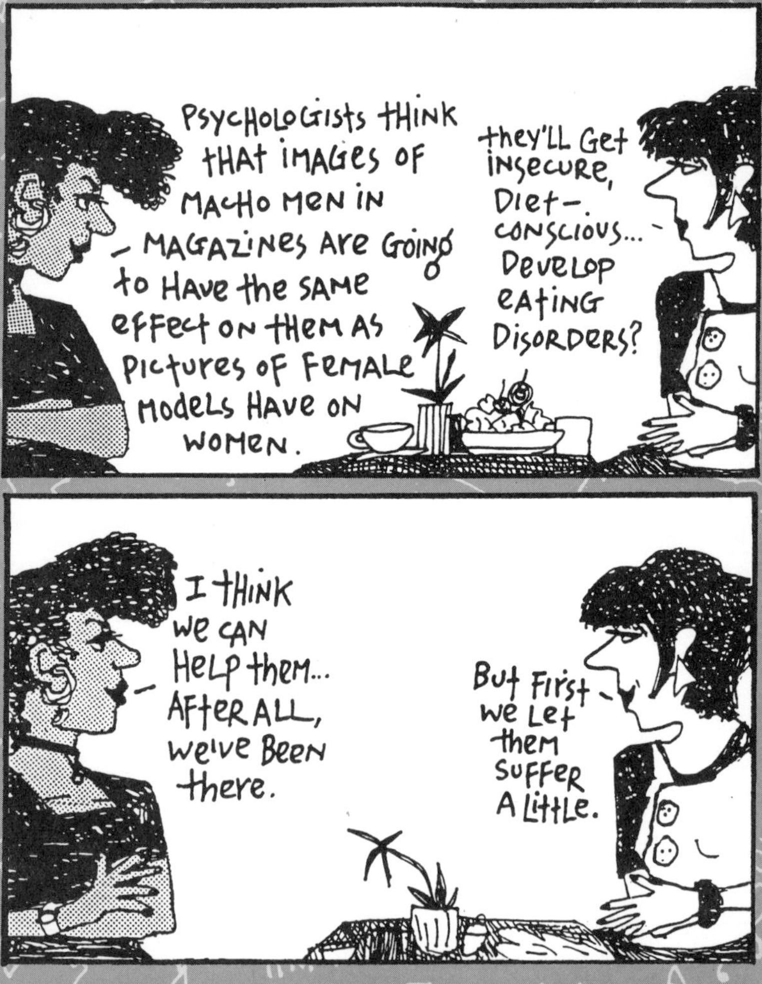

# My Grandmother, the Goddess

Recently I received a letter from a magazine inviting me to submit any new manuscripts I might wish to have considered for publication. A civilized and caring request, I thought, but one that was followed by a stern warning: they did not publish doggerel, sentimentality, or ancestor worship.

Right away I thought of my mother's mother, who was a goddess, and the time she took me shopping for my first party dress. Bessie lived with my grandfather on the third floor of the building where my parents and I lived. Bessie and I spent a lot of time in each other's company. We often took baths together and played a game she invented called "The *Titanic*." My grandmother would wrap her huge arms around me and rock us both back and forth rapidly until the water in the tub resembled enormous waves.

Then she would shout, "Man overboard, save the women and children first!" This would never fail to amuse me and we continued to bathe together until I was twenty-seven.

Anyway, on a lovely spring day she took me on a shopping trip downtown to the Fair department store. I was six years old, and my wardrobe consisted mainly of striped overalls and T-shirts. I had never seen so many dresses in one place before; I was overwhelmed and on the verge of hysteria. Painfully, I narrowed my choices down to two dresses, each wonderful in its own way, and I vacillated from one to the other like a yo-yo.

MYSELF AT SIX

Finally, I drew a deep breath and picked the one that was covered with little flower sprigs.

the DRESS

My grandmother left the dressing room to hang up the pink, dotted swiss dress with the sweetheart neckline and the three-tiered skirt and the tiny rosebud at the waist, and as soon as she did I knew that was the dress of my dreams, the one I would need in order to finish college, marry the teaching assistant in my sociology class, divorce him, move to California, and eventually become a syndicated cartoonist and playwright. Somehow I communicated this to my grandmother and she and I ran as one from the dressing room to get that dress back before it was too late.

It appeared to be too late. A strange woman was examining the dress in a proprietary way. I held my breath as my grandmother approached her. Bessie was a big woman; she had owned her own dry goods store, she fitted corsets for a living, and she had a certain field marshal's authority in her bearing. She spoke to the woman in an amazingly detached voice, considering all that was riding on her mission. "Did you know,"

the tub with waves

she said, "that the dots on that dress will fall off the minute you wash it?" The woman flung the dress from her as you would a snake, and we rushed home with it. I put it on immediately and my grandfather and I danced around the living room with my skirt twirling in graceful arcs until dinnertime.

# Mother/Daughter Outfits

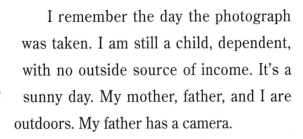

MY, DON'T YOU LOOK ADORABLE.

I remember the day the photograph was taken. I am still a child, dependent, with no outside source of income. It's a sunny day. My mother, father, and I are outdoors. My father has a camera.

Mother and I are dressed in identical forest-green jumpers, their wide flat collars edged with tiny felt leaves in autumn colors. Mothers and daughters used to dress alike. Not long ago I saw a catalog, mercifully thin, of identical outerwear for the entire family. Mom, Dad, and the two kids wearing the same ski jackets. It chilled me to the core.

Anyway, it is a crisp, sunny fall day, and my mother and I are wearing our adorable forest-green jumpers with light-colored blouses underneath and my father is documenting the event on the grass parkway in front of our building.

Suddenly I experience the first stirrings of independence. My mother and I are wearing mother/daughter outfits, but I want to be photographed alone. My mother finds this unnatural. I insist that one of these pictures be taken of me in front of the big tree, by myself. My mother is still unresponsive. Possibly I hold my breath and let my eyes roll back in my head until she says to my dad, "Okay, okay, go ahead, take her picture alone."

the tree

Dad takes my picture. I have that photograph. It haunts my dreams. I am standing in front of the big tree smiling charmingly, proud and adult, while in the background my mother leans out from behind the tree, a victorious grin on her face. Through the years I have dreamt that photograph, rows and rows of mothers and daughters dressed identically... variations on the theme of getting what I want and having it snatched from me. In my waking hours I am my own person; in my dreams, my mother always jumps out from behind that tree.

But wait, I do have a sentimental memory of my mother. It's the fifties

the MotheR/DAUGHteR Contest

and I am an art student at the University of Illinois. During a Mother's Day Weekend at college, my dormitory throws a mother/daughter look-alike contest. In the evening we gather in the living room of the dormitory for the judging. Looking around, Mom and I are taken aback. We realize there are many mothers and daughters who look more alike than we do. We want to win. We do not speak; there is no time to consider a strategy.

When the judges stop in front of us, we put aside our conflicts, our history of disappointing one another, and reaffirming our deep connection for one brilliant moment, we make the same hideous face simultaneously and win, hands down.

# On the Menopause Express

It's a movie in black and white.... A woman runs through the narrow corridor, buffeted back and forth by the motion of the train, the countryside whizzing by blurred, feature-less. Sinister men with flat faces shoulder her aside in the narrow corridor. She is breathless — wide-eyed with desperation. She's looking for someone, a stranger. The stranger will know her. Her face is the password.

With her last ounce of strength, she flings open the door to the club car. She rakes the room with her ravaged gaze. There are two men with bright red faces and tiny matching mustaches drinking gin, a teenager with a straw hanging out of his nose, a young couple with a small dog, and four elderly women playing mah-jongg. She whirls around, searching each face for a sign. No hope there, or there.... Her feverish eyes fall on a woman in an Armani suit reading an ancient copy of *Lear's* magazine. She screams, "Can someone open a damn window? I'm sweating bullets."

People avert their eyes. They pretend not to notice her outburst. The well-dressed woman with the expensive haircut reading *Lear's* smiles to herself and slowly raises her insolent gaze. "Don't be a fool. I have what you need," she says, and places one tiny, shiny, brownish-red football-shaped pill in the woman's palm and hands her a glass of champagne. "...But it'll cost you."

# Why I gave up feminism

GIVING UP
FEMINISM
MADE MY HAIR
THICKER AND
MY CLEAVAGE
QUITE PRONOUNCED.
I HIGHLY
RECOMMEND IT.

I'm in tune with my times. It's my first experience with being like other people, and boy does it feel good.

I feel ten pounds lighter since I gave up feminism. I was tired of dragging around our history and being such a pain in the butt to myself and others. Feminism ruined the movies for me. You know if you're a feminist there's only one movie you can like and even *Thelma & Louise* is a little too heavy on the violence to really qualify.

I used to stay at home and watch worthwhile documentaries on my VCR. I didn't get out much and when I did I fought with everyone.

Now, postfeminist, I can watch what I like and my hair is Drew Barrymore blond and I can hang out in mixed company and no one ever seems stupid or irritating or a waste of time and I have lots of nice relationships with very old men. I don't mind getting their prescriptions refilled, either.

And I'm done with blaming capitalism for poverty and violence. I embrace the idea that television and single mothers are responsible for the breakdown of society and multiple killings in fast food restaurants.

I enjoy saying "repressed memory" and "pork barrel" and "Hillary" in a voice dripping with sarcasm and ennui. I must admit I had the voice when I was a strident, whining, victim-type feminist, but now I can make my lip curl when I say "Public Radio." I've even started to look a bit like William Buckley, but that's not all bad.

I've grown to appreciate Orrin Hatch's arid allure. I think Bob Dole is darkly witty and saturninely sexy. I think Jesse Helms has Southern baby-boy charm. I'm a softy for Pat Buchanan's dark-angel side and I think Newt has really nice hair.... I'm afraid I still have a bit of trouble with Rush Limbaugh.

I watched too many of those 1950s science fiction movies as a kid. I see Rush as a blobby pod person. I can't get into him. It's not to my credit. When I hear his voice, my Dr. Strangelove arm reaches out, of its own volition, to change the station. Don't touch that dial.

It's kind of an aesthetic knee-jerk gag reaction and I'm trying to get over it. I've even organized a support group for watching his TV show. Whenever my old feminazi self reaches for the remote control, one of my codependents whacks me with it. Thank you, please do it again.

And I've discovered that I like renouncing things. It's the trait that truly puts me in sync with my times. I am so nineties. I positively tingle at the thought of giving something up. I look forward to developing an allergy to my cats. I revel in discussing the minutiae of my doctor-mandated relinquishing of saturated fat. I obsess at the grocery store. It takes me hours to shop. I really study the menu at a restaurant now.... Before I would simply glance at it and say, "Bring me the barbecued ribs... a half order, I have to save room for dessert."

My only regret is that I can't give up smoking. It has so much potential in the self-righteousness category. Better than drugs, I think... maybe even better than alcohol. When you stop drinking you don't get to tell your mother she has to drink her chardonnay out on the porch.

Alas, I was never a smoker. I never drank to excess. I have never been fat. No, I'm not bragging. In fact it makes me feel inadequate. I've never done a 12-step program for anything and I feel inferior to those who have. I didn't do est — I heard they made you wait to pee. I was into control then; now I'm willing to give it over to a higher power.

If I hadn't been neurotic for most of my adult life, I wouldn't have had

anything to look back on. As it is, I think I might have to develop a coke habit or a sexual addiction in order to have something to give up.

Thanks to being neurotic I've experienced individual therapy, encounter groups, and group therapy. I won't embarrass myself in a 12-step program.

I was good in group therapy. I liked telling my story to a whole new bunch of people. I'd probably do real well in a 12-step program... if I can ever find something to give up. On the other hand, I really don't like to tell any story over and over, and I get bored easily, especially with my own life.

I'd probably have to join a new group every few months. Kind of a cowboy, transient, mobile-home kind of thing. In my new group I could reinvent myself ... synthesize my life and the lives of friends into an arresting history of suffering. A composite confessional.

Is that cheating? Using the stuff of others' lives to enhance your own... Kind of a vampirish thing to do. Now, there's something I could get my teeth into. First of all, I wouldn't actually have to drink anyone's blood. I'd just say I did. Allude to it. Not many reformed vampires around to point a long bony finger at me and say I got the details wrong... plus I've seen all the movies.

Vampirism. An addiction that would be difficult — but not, I think, impossible — to find a 12-step program for.

Spokesmen for the Right Wing of the Republican Party Are trying to Associate the Democrats with a so-called Feminist Agenda... one that causes women to...

Leave their husbands, kill their children, Practice witchcraft, Destroy Capitalism, and become Lesbians.

Heavy schedule.

BAD GIRLS!

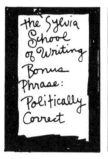

the Sylvia School of Writing Bonus Phrase: Politically Correct

CLYDE was slumped in a kitchen chair, looking dazed. "I don't think feminism is so bad," he said. "And I'm kinda interested in non-western civilizations." "How do you feel about Bush's Attitude toward a Civil Rights Bill?" I asked cautiously. "I think he doesn't want one, no matter how watered down," he answered, looking surprised. "OH MY GOD, CLYDE," I screamed, "I think you've got P.C." "Get my pills," he gasped falling off his chair.

Remember all-male bars? A hundred guys standing crowded together at lunchtime, drinking beer and eating corned beef sandwiches on big slabs of rye bread. You knew you were a guy because you were there.

PLACING-the-BLAME SQUARELY –

Paradise.

the Feminists Destroyed those Bars. Now you have to travel to the woods and beat Drums with a bunch of wusses to prove you're a man. I hate it.

WHERE-IT-BELONGS THERAPY.

Feminists Have a lot to Answer For.

**137**

# Notes from the traveler who Whines

I like to travel in my bathrobe.

Well, a really bad trip is where you die, am I right? Anything less: dysentery, loss of your passport, bugged hotel rooms, insects the size of ponies, mud slides, frostbite, and outright rudeness are the stuff of good stories when you get back home. The recollection of near disaster is the only thing that will remove the glassy look from a friend's eyes as you recount your trip to Afghanistan or Iowa. Well, I'm not doing it. It's not worth it.

James Morris was with Edmund Hillary when he reached the summit of Mount Everest. That same intrepid man later had a sex change operation and became Jan Morris. Fearful journeys, both, but Ms. Morris is addicted to exploring and has never had a bad experience.

I have had bad experiences in Elmhurst, Illinois. Like soufflé, I do not travel well. I whine. My IQ goes down. I forget to look both ways. I can get lost taking a new way home from the office. London defeated me. I panic over trifles. I became comatose in a hotel in Santa Monica because there was an odd stain on the ceiling and the spreads felt clammy. I had to be half-carried to the plane. (A plane, oh my God, I'm on a plane. Well, it was either that or live in Santa Monica forever.)

So I am unable to visit the rain forest, take a solo trip around the globe in a tiny boat, or see the pyramids in old Algiers. I will never exchange courteous speech and gifts with chieftains in Samoa or get a haircut in Kashmir. If I were by profession a governess, you would not find me in a forbidding mansion on a moor in a windswept corner of England, even though I was down on my luck and the master of the house was terribly good-looking and stern.

I am an armchair traveler of a very limited kind. I like to read books about awful trips. I loved *Forgotten Fatherland*. The author searches for the lost colony of Elisabeth Nietzsche in Paraguay and suffers mightily from aggressive biting insects and a diet composed solely of protein. The English seem to excel at this kind of writing. Bless them. I keep a copy of *Bad Trips* (edited by Keith Fraser) at my bedside. I leaf through it when I feel the urge to travel. It calms me and confirms to me the rightness of my abject wimpiness. Even for armchair traveling I impose strict limits. I don't watch films in which young people are imprisoned in Turkey for minor drug offenses or where women disguise themselves in chadors and escape with their daughters from alien cultures. Makes me nervous.

Most trips involve plane travel. I hate that. A friend of mine was offered a free trip to Uzbekistan. She couldn't pass it up. Well, who could? Many of us have longed to go to a theater festival in Uzbekistan all our adult lives. She said she thought of me when, on the second or fifth leg of the journey, her plane, experiencing mechanical difficulties, landed at an unmarked airfield. After quite a while, in which no one in authority communicated anything and the passengers were not allowed off the aircraft, a long ladder was placed against the wing. A man climbed up the ladder and hit something sharply with a hammer and they took off again.

the Sylvia School of Writing:

"HAD I BUT KNOWN..." Students, PLEASE WRITE 600 MORE WORDS AND use the BONUS PHRASE: "Surely there's some mistake..."

"HAD I BUT KNOWN THAT RUNNING OUT FOR STARBUCKS COFFEE AT THE CRACK OF DAWN WOULD LEAD ME INTO THE ARMS OF A MAN WHO WAS LEAVING THAT MORNING TO SEARCH FOR the LOST COLONY OF NEW GERMANIA IN PARAGUAY, AND THAT I WOULD ACCOMPANY HIM WEARING A PINK SWEATSUIT AND SLING-BACK SANDALS, I WOULD HAVE MADE INSTANT."

Rita, Do we HAVE ANY DECENT COFFEE?

WE'VE GOT ALMOND-MOCHA OR NACHO-MINT.

the Woman who does Everything More Beautifully than you travels Better too.

OCTOBER 1993. I WAS WRITING IN MY JOURNAL, WAITING TO BOARD THE FLIGHT TO PARIS WHEN A DISTINGUISHED-LOOKING MAN WALKED UP TO ME AND HANDED ME HIS FIRST-CLASS TICKET. HE KISSED MY HAND AND MURMURED, "A WOMAN AS LOVELY AS YOU SHOULDN'T HAVE TO FLY COACH," THEN HE MELTED INTO THE CROWD. IT WAS QUITE TOUCHING, REALLY, BUT UNNECESSARY... I ALWAYS FLY FIRST-CLASS.

Hi, this is YOUR PILOT. We're SOMETHING LIKE 124th IN LINE FOR TAKEOFF. So I'M GOING to PULL OUT TO THE LEFT RATHER QUICKLY, PRESS THE PEDAL TO THE METAL AND GET TO THE FRONT OF THE LINE AND TAKE OFF BEFORE ANYONE KNOWS WHAT'S HAPPENING... ARE YOU WITH ME?

PHOTO: JENNIFER GIRARD

Nicole Hollander lives and works in Chicago...
she is never far from her bathtub, her cats or her fax.